*Lautrec*

**Phidal**

"It is one of the wonderful privileges of art that the artist's expression of horror and pain, if rhythmic and cadenced, fill the spirit with a calm joy."

Charles Baudelaire

"Bébé Lou Pouliot" in the patois of Albi means pretty baby. This was the nickname given to Henri de Toulouse-Lautrec at his birth, and it expresses how much the child was desired and charming. The painter was born on November 24, 1864 at the Hôtel Bosc, Rue de l'Ecole-Mage in the heart of the medieval town of Albi, in south-western France. He descended from one of the noblest and wealthiest families of France. Henri's two grandmothers were sisters and his birth strengthened this existing bond between the two most influential families of the region, the Toulouse-Lautrecs and the Tapié de Céleyrans. He was christened Henri in honor of Henri V, the legitimist pretender to the throne of France, grandson of Charles X. A charming and high-spirited child, his sunny and sweet character entranced his whole family: "Henri chirps from morning to night," one of his grandmothers wrote. "He goes on like a cricket who brings joy to the entire household. Each time he must go away, we feel an immense void, for he takes the place of twenty people here."

Rich and spoiled, Toulouse-Lautrec grew up in an atmosphere of luxury, where nothing was denied him. Besides, of the Tapié and Lautrec families, nobody had to work for a living; rather they pursued their interests, with skill and intelligence. Thus, his father, a sculptor by profession, spent a good part of the year in Paris, where he also became a keen student of exotic peoples and their customs. A true eccentric, one day he returned to Albi dressed as a Kirghiz tribesman, and for a time he even lived in a tent in order to understand this Asiatic people's way of life.

Henri's charm, gaiety and intelligence stayed with him as he grew; he received a fine upbringing, and passed his days in blissful security, drawing, horseback riding, and studying English and Latin with his mother. He was sent off to Paris to continue his studies at the Lycée Condorcet, where he made friends with a fellow student, Maurice Joyant. It was a bond that would last his lifetime. Though Henri was active in sports, he was frail and by the time he was ten years old, his delicate health required a milder climate. The town of Nice was decided upon, and he was withdrawn from the Parisian school.

In spite of his faltering health, Henri's brilliant personality did not fade, and during their trip to Nice, his grandmother wrote to Countess Adèle that "his bright disposition has not abandoned him, so that his good spirits keep at the same pitch even when he is alone. He is still too young to go hunting with the gentlemen here, though he is plucky and clever and never shrinks before obstacles that are much too great for him."

During this period, the breach between his parents deepened and their separation became inevitable. Henri must have suffered greatly

*Nude Woman before a Mirror - 1897. Private collection, USA*

at this, though he wrote roguishly: "My father, the count, his only sprees are on *café au lait*!" In 1878 Henri had a bad fall and broke his leg. Fifteen months later, another accident resulting in a new fracture aggravated his state of health. Sadly, he was crippled for life. Henri described the incident in a letter to a friend: "I fell from a low chair onto the floor and broke my left thighbone. But now, thank God, it has mended and I am starting to walk with a crutch with someone to help me." His father wrote of the second fracture that it "was due to a fall not much more severe while out walking with his mother. He fell into a ravine that was not more that four or five feet deep. While his mother went to look for a doctor, he stayed calm and did not despair. He stayed seated on the ground and held his leg straight with both hands."

In fact, it now appears that these accidents were the consequence of a serious disease, little known at the time: polyepiphyseal dystrophy.

This involves the underdevelopment of certain bone tissues that leaves the bones in a very brittle state. At the age of thirteen Henri was a boy of average height: four feet eleven inches. As an adult he was just over five feet tall.

Far from sinking into despair, the boy's strength of character surprised those close to him, and, following unavoidable surgery, he wrote to a friend: "The surgical crime was perpetrated on Monday, and the fracture, so admirable from a surgical point of view (not from mine, clearly understood!) saw the light of day. The doctor was thrilled and left me in peace until this morning. Then, under the false pretext of setting me on my feet, he had me bend my leg at a right angle, making me suffer something fierce. Oh! Would that you were here for just five little minutes a day! Then I could face my future suffering with serenity!" And when anybody sympathized with him, he joked: "It's no use crying over me. I don't deserve it. It was so clumsy of me. I've had ever so many visitors and I'm getting terribly spoiled."

In July 1881, in Paris after one of his many stays at the seaside, he took his baccalauréat examination. Unhappily, he failed and had to work hard throughout the holidays to try again in the fall. This time, he succeeded, and wrote the good news to a friend: "Caught up in the whirl of the baccalauréat, this time I managed to pass. I neglected my friends, painting and all that's worth anything in this world to pour over my dictionaries and trusty textbooks. In the end, the Toulouse examining board found me acceptable, in spite of the nonsensical answers I blurted out to their questions. I made citations of Lucretius that do not exist, and the professor, wishing to appear erudite swallowed it all whole. Finally, it's over with. You will find my prose somewhat limp, but it is the post-examination let-down that follows so much tension. Let's hope for some improvement the next time!"

At sixteen, drawing was already a passion for him. Henri's first teacher was René Princeteau, a family friend who was a great specialist in painting horses. Later, the student showed more talent that the master, and the honest Princeteau advised the family to have Henri further his training at the atelier of Léon Bonnat, one of the most celebrated painters in Paris at the time. Describing his experience with Bonnat, Lautrec wrote to his uncle Charles: "You are probably curious to know what kind of encouragement Bonnat offers me. He tells me: 'Your painting is not bad; it is rather modish, but still, it's not bad. But your drawing is plainly atrocious.' And I must buckle down and start afresh, plowing ahead."

When he was eighteen, Henri enrolled in the atelier of Cormon. Cormon was a painter then very much in vogue, whose academic *Cain*, inspired by Victor Hugo's *La légende des Siècles*, met with resounding success at the 1880 Salon. About Cormon, Henri Rachou, one of Henri's friends at the atelier, wrote: "I never saw him make a mistake in his assessment of one of us. He was incredibly insightful, and was never indulgent except with those for whom he felt some friendship, treating the others with a bluntness bordering on cruelty. When he wished, his manners were impeccable, and he showed a precise sense of decorum, adapting himself to any environment. I have never seen him either exalted or in the grips of ambition. He was, before everything, an artist." At the atelier, Toulouse-Lautrec met Vincent van Gogh with whom he shared a lifelong bond of friendship. Unlike the Impressionists, Lautrec was not at all drawn to landscapes; the almost exclusive subject of his painting was the human figure, because, according to the critic Jacques Lassaigne, "it offered him the freedom to use his gift of observation, his verve. His magnificently tense, nervous stroke and his skill as a colourist were the tools for an essentially psychological exploration, keen, often harsh, indeed implacable.

His painting offers no hint of compassion, but rather a sense of discretion. And if by chance he felt caught in a trap, he used his irony to extricate himself. Of all his works, only the portraits of his mother have a

secret vibration that betrays the overwhelming love he felt for her." In the same period, Toulouse-Lautrec and his dauber friends frequented the cabarets, especially that of the songster Aristide Bruant, whose spirit delighted them.

*You pack of abortions and half-baked fools!*
*What cross-breeds are you*
*if your mums had no bubs and your fathers no tools?*
*Were you suckled on asses' milk,*
*so you're still in the rough?*
*Here we'll admit none of such ilk*
*it's up to your parents to finish the job and show their stuff!*

With ditties such as this Aristide Bruant welcomed his customers to Le Mirliton, a tiny cabaret in Boulevard de Rochechouart where he sang sentimental ballads or anarchistic anthems in a loud and booming voice.

Toulouse-Lautrec decorated the Mirliton with pictures illustrating Aristide's songs, such as his drawing of Nini-peau-de-chien (Dog-skin Nini), the heroine of the song *A la bastille*. The ringleader of Cormon's atelier was unquestionably Grenier, who together with his pretty wife Lily, had utterly charmed Toulouse-Lautrec.

The artist was not at all interested in professional models, rather, it was life that inspired and attracted him. "One day when he and Rachou were on their way to lunch at Boivains," wrote Gauzi, "they passed a young woman dressed simply like a factory girl, but who had such a head of copper-coloured hair that Lautrec stopped in his tracks and eagerly cried out: 'She's fantastic! Look how she glows! If only she would pose for me, it would be wonderful! You've got to ask her!' Her name was Carmen Gaudin. She was a sweet working girl, a little bit delicate. Lautrec, who had imagined her to be a terrific bitch, was surprised to learn that her lover beat her black and blue. She was very punctual and for a long time remained his favourite model." At the hand of Lautrec, Carmen was to become a splendid *Laundress* and Rose la Rouge, the heroine of another of Bruant's songs, *A Montrouge*.

Thanks to his old classmate Maurice Joyant, who in the meantime had become an art dealer, as well as editor of the review *Paris Illustré*, Lautrec started contributing regularly to *Le Courrier Français*, and this was the beginning of a lengthy collaboration in which the two experimented with printing techniques.

Such serious work, however, did not slow Lautrec and friends' nocturnal rhythms in the least. Though they did not abandon the Mirliton, they could often be seen at the Moulin de la Galette dance hall, which had changed a great deal since Renoir's time: it had become an arena for streetwalkers and their pimps and it was there that Lautrec first saw "La Goulue" dance. He and his friends could also be seen at the Chat Noir, a more sophisticated haunt of poets and songwriters, or in the new club that had opened on Boulevard de Clichy, at the foot of Montmartre, Le Moulin Rouge. This new place headlined the likes of "Cha-U-Kao", the clowness in a Japanese guise, whose name was a play on words (Chahut — or Shindy — Chaos); the Macarona circus acrobat whose portrait Lautrec did a number of times: Jane Avril, nicknamed "La Mélinite", of whom Joyant said "She dances like an orchid in ecstasy"; and last, but not least, La Goulue — a subject who enchanted the painter. Louise Weber, nicknamed La Goulue or the Glutton, was a 16-year-old girl when Lautrec first saw her dance at the Moulin Rouge. Yvette Guilbert, the highly talented actress and chanteuse and sincere friend of Lautrec, drew this vivid portrait of the showgirl: "La Goulue wore black silk stockings, and with her black satin-shoed foot in one hand would set spinning round her the sixty metres of lace skirts she wore so that her panties showed: these were whimsically embroidered with a heart that roguishly stretched across her tiny bottom when she took her cheeky bows; her adorable legs, nimble, sprightly and alluring would appear and disappear from behind tufts of pink ribbons at her knees with a darling froth of lace reaching to her slender ankles. With a smart little kick, the dancer would knock off her partner's hat, and then she would do splits, her torso erect in a tight little sky-blue blouse and her black satin skirt opening out like an umbrella, spreading for five metres around her.

She was stunning! La Goulue was pretty and rakishly witty to look at; blonde, a fringe of bangs fell over her forehead straight down to her eyebrows. She wore her hair twisted high up on her head and coiled tightly at the nape of her neck so that it would stay in place during her numbers. From her temples the classic lovelocks hung down in ringlets over her ears, and from Paris to New York, via London's East End slums, all the girls of the period wanted to wear their hair like hers and with that same coloured ribbon knotted at their necks."

It was in this period that Lautrec was commissioned by the Moulin Rouge to design their new poster. He had just turned twenty-six, and though he was inexperienced in this form of art, he discovered the key to modern advertising: simple, arresting images. His design was accepted; it showed La Goulue in the foreground and the words "Moulin Rouge" in eye-catching letters repeated three times.

In 1892, Bruant starred in a show at the Ambassadeurs, an exclusive café-concert on the Champs-Elysées. He insisted that his friend Lautrec — by then a highly successful poster artist — design the showbill. The club manager Ducare strongly objected to the result. "Take that frightful thing — that trash — down!" he cried when he saw it for the first time. Bruant answered him: "My dear man, you will leave that poster exactly where it is, and moreover you will slap them up on each side of the stage... and listen to me well, if by quarter to eight — not eight o'clock, mind you — this has not been done, I won't go on! Is that clear?"

"At the stated hour," wrote Joyant, "the poster was in place onstage, framing Bruant. Both the singer and the poster were an enormous success. After the show, Ducare admitted to having been mistaken."

When Lautrec designed a poster for a music-hall called the Divan Japonais, it was Jane Avril who occupied the foreground. He used her image again on a poster announcing her reappearance at the Jardin de Paris, and later in one for a show — that did not meet with much success — in London.

May Belfort was Lautrec's next new subject. She was not as pretty as Jane, but her strong features were unusual. Finally, the great Loïe Fuller took her place in Lautrec's art. She danced waving veils on long rods, in a scintillating halo of changing coloured lights produced with modern electrical projectors. For her poster, Toulouse-Lautrec invented a new lithographic technique, colouring the print by hand and sprinkling it with gold dust so that just the shadows of the dancer's head and hands were visible amid the iridescent glow of her voluminous veils.

Though his career as a poster artist was flourishing, Lautrec did not forget his love of painting. His ties with Cormon had worn thin, but he did not stop exhibiting at Bruant's cabaret and at the Mirliton, the Tambourin with Van Gogh, and at the Cercle Volney, an exclusive club, as well as in Belgium, several times.

Lautrec kept company with a very diverse crowd. First of all, there was his mother — whom he loved dearly — who lived in a very bourgeois apartment in the Rue Victor Macé, not far from Lautrec's studio. Lautrec often dined with her, bringing along his friends. Then, there were the brothels. The painter often disappeared from his home, carrying trunks with him as if leaving on a long journey. In truth, his absences lasted only a couple of weeks and the hackney coach stopped just a few hundred yards down the road, in Rue Richelieu or Rue des Moulins, in front of one of those "houses" that the bourgeois mentality pretended to disapprove.

One day, a man of high social rank was seated with his mistress at a table near Lautrec's in a restaurant. The man asked him in a loud voice: "How can you live in such places?" Lautrec replied: "Heaven knows you, sir, prefer to entertain the claque in your own home!"

The painter loved the residents of these "maisons". The aristocratic scion of one of the oldest families of French nobility, Lautrec saw no difference, from a social point of view between a streetwalker and a nouveau riche. There was nothing vulgar or of questionable taste in the paintings he did in these houses; it was not his intention to shock. The ladies called him "monsieur Henri, the painter".

"Among these women," wrote Francis Jourdain, "Lautrec is a sort of spoiled child, sweetly tyrannical. They appreciate his simplicity and his way of playing down his rising fame and his illustrious family name. His companions would be embarrassed if they sensed in him any condescension or the ridiculous desire to act the gangster, the tough guy. He is what he is."

Lautrec's favourite was Mireille. She appears in profile in the foreground of the large painting In the Salon. "They're trying to take me for a ride," he confided once to Gauzi. "They hide Mireille when I ask for her, even though I've made up my mind to pay her for a day off. I write her and she never fails to come see me. She was here yesterday." Then he pointed to a bunch of violets. "That's Mireille's doing. She bought it on her way here to see me and sweetly gave it to me."

The period in which Lautrec habited the "maisons" was, artistically speaking, his most fertile phase, when he painted his greatest masterpieces. From 1892-94, in addition to his paintings, his output included a number of lithographs, his finest posters, several illustrations for books and periodicals, as well as some stage scenery.

*Portrait of Maurice Joyant - 1900. Musée Henri de Toulouse-Lautrec, Albi*

At around the same time, his childhood friend Maurice Joyant succeeded Théo van Gogh (Vincent's brother) as manager of the Goupil Gallery, and, after much hesitation, Lautrec was finally persuaded to hold his first exhibition there. To his surprise, the press was not hostile, and the exhibition was even honoured by a visit from Degas. "One evening at around six," wrote Joyant, "Degas appeared, wrapped in his Inverness cape. He proceeded to examine with care all the pictures, all the while humming a little tune to himself. He wound his way around the entire exhibition without saying a word. He had started down the spiral staircase when he turned back, and with just his head and shoulders popping up from the narrow stairwell he said to Lautrec, who was standing there shy and anxious: 'Well Lautrec, I can see that you're one of us'. I can still see Lautrec beaming with inner satisfaction at this casual nod of approval."

To avoid scandal, the paintings with the "maisons" as their subject matter were hung in a room closed to the public, on view only to friends and connoisseurs who had obtained prior permission.

A year later, Durand-Ruel showed a set of lithographs by Lautrec on the occasion of a Manet exhibition.

The last exhibition organized during the artist's lifetime was held at the Goupil Gallery in London, in 1898.

Wine, spirits, sleepness nights and debauchery had taken their toll on Toulouse-Lautrec's already delicate health. One morning he awoke from a night of revelry in a room with barred windows and a padlocked door at the psychiatric clinic of Neuilly, called the "St. James' Folly". The artist was far from being mad. His family and friends had mistaken for madness the over-excitable nervous state that he had been in for some time.

Clearly, Toulouse-Lautrec's health had been deteriorating daily. In February 1899, he had a fit of delirium tremens and in the fall broke his collarbone. A detoxification cure seemed to be urgently required. Among his friends, only Joyant objected, but in vain. When the painter came to, he was seized with anguish. He wrote to his father: "Papa, here's your chance to do a gentlemanly deed. I am locked up and everything that is locked up dies." But his father did not dare to interfere and he continued his lonely struggle.

Fifteen days later, he was released from the clinic on probation, with the order to stay in his room. Happy to have regained some semblance of freedom, he started working again. When Joyant commissioned a series of circus illustrations from him, he produced from his sickroom a truly exceptional set of drawings in coloured pencil. The doctors were impressed by his progress and wrote: "M. Henri de Toulouse-Lautrec has calmed down greatly and is in quite a different state from that in which we found him during our previous visits ... It is certain that this recent improvement can only last if the patient is kept in the same conditions of physical and mental hygiene for a period of several weeks ..." And on May 17: "The patient continues to improve physically and mentally ... The symptoms of delirium have not recurred. Signs of alcoholic intoxication, apart from slight trembling, are hardly noticeable ... But owing to his amnesia, unstable character and lack of willpower, it is necessary to keep M. Henri de Toulouse-Lautrec under constant observation." On May 20 he was definitively set free. He went to Normandy to convalesce and stayed for four months in Le Havre. At the end of July he left Le Havre for Bordeaux, and then spent a few months with his mother at the Château de Malromé en Gironde. In the fall, he returned definitively to Paris. From then until the beginning of 1900, Toulouse-Lautrec worked unremittingly. His technique changed markedly: he now used a heavy impasto on wood panels and canvas, and his palette darkened. One of his favourite models at this time was Madame Poupoule, a plump demi-mondaine whom he painted at her dressing table or standing at the foot of her bed. But his absolute favourite was Maurice Joyant's young and pretty girlfriend, Louise. The poet Paul Leclercq thus described Toulouse-Lautrec's rapport with women: "Lautrec adored the company of women, and the more illogical, scatterbrained, impulsive and crazier they were, the more he enjoyed them, provided they were natural, for Lautrec liked to bring out the personality of each individual, and he was interested and amused by the freshness and naïveté of the direct images formed by their little minds. The passing mistress of one of his friends remained for a long time one of his closest companions. She was a young seamstress and model (or *margouin* in Parisian slang), with luxuriant blond hair and a pert little squirrel face. He called her 'Croque-si-Margouin', or 'Pretty-enough-to-eat'. They were like two children at play together. They understood each other. What he felt for his women friends was a strange mixture of jovial comradery and repressed desire. And since he was conscious of his inferiority, and yet like Cyrano knew nothing of petty jealousy, when he appreciated a woman, he refrained from showing his true feelings, and his greatest joy was for her to be appreciated, in the full sense of the word, by one of his friends."

In 1900 a slump in wine sales forced Lautrec's mother to reduce his allowance. He was not only humiliated by this, but also inconvenienced. That year, he left sooner than usual for Normandy. In Honfleur, at the request of Lucien Guitry, he illustrated his last theatre programme. An idle summer on the Bay of Arcachon restored some strength to him — enough to return to Paris to be with his friends and put his studio in order. This was to be his last stay in the capital; he seemed to sense that he was going to die. As if on a pilgrimage, he looked up the persons and the places he had most loved. When he left for Arcachon in July, nobody had any illusions — it was a farewell. In August the Countess de Toulouse-Lautrec took her half-paralyzed son back to the Château de Malromé, for it was there among the arbors of his youth that the painter wished to end his days. Henri de Toulouse-Lautrec died on September 9, 1901 at the age of thirty-six.

*At Les Ambassadeurs. Multicolor gravure.* Le Figaro Illustré, *July 1893*

1. Self-Portrait of Henri de Toulouse-Lautrec - 1880. Musée Henri de Toulouse-Lautrec, Albi - *Painted when he was seventeen years old, this portrait shows the artist's precocious talent. His vocation had been evident since his childhood and he applied himself to it with verve and originality to the end.*

2. The Mail-Coach - 1881. Musée du Petit Palais, Paris - *Toulouse-Lautrec's natural style was already evident in this first portrait of his father. Lautrec had just turned sixteen when he did it, and was studying under the painter Princeteau, a friend of the family and great specialist in the painting of horses.*

3. The Countess Adèle de Toulouse-Lautrec at Malromé - 1883. Musée Henri de Toulouse-Lautrec, Albi - *This portrait of his mother was painted at Malromé one summer when Toulose-Lautrec was studying under Bonnat. The different visual planes of the broad and simple figure accentuate her serene expression and thoughtful air. The painter felt a loving veneration for his mother which emerges clearly in this canvas.*

4. Tethered Horse - c. 1881. Private collection, Paris - *Toulouse-Lautrec's first real teacher was René Princeteau, a family friend and great painter of horses. When he worked with Princeteau, Toulouse-Lautrec did several paintings of horses, jockeys and races, as well as simply animals themselves.*

5. At the Circus Fernando: the Ringmaster - 1880. The Art Institute of Chicago - *This is one of the first paintings in which the expressive force and innovative cleverness of the artist's compositions clearly emerges. The first in a series dedicated to the circus, it is one of the earliest examples of the original artistic devices adopted by the painter: the raised point of view, silhouettes captured in dynamic moments, synthetic outlines, colour applied in flat and uniform areas.*

6. The Laundress - 1889. Private collection, Paris - *Drawn to ordinary life in his work, Toulouse-Lautrec did not like to paint professional models. This young woman is Carmen Gaudin, a factory girl who enchanted the artist from the moment he glimpsed her on a busy street. Under his paintbrush, she became this splendid laundress, as well as "Rosa la Rouge", the heroine of the song "A Montrouge".*

7. Girl with Red Hair - 1889. Bührle Collection, Zurich - *This is one of several portraits that the painter did in the public park of Montmartre. The natural setting serves only as a backdrop, but the girl's expression shows the painter's vibrant sensitivity. Toulouse-Lautrec's models were rarely professionals, and the painter preferred to allow himself to be seduced by chance encounters.*

8. The Painter Henri Rachou - c. 1882. Algur H. Meadows Collection, Dallas - *Though he had not yet moved away from his teacher Cormon's method, at this time Toulouse-Lautrec met the other students at the atelier. This painting shows the influence of this group of young painters, who emerged as the most important forces in French modern art.*

9. Portrait of Hélène Vary - 1888. Kunsthalle, Bremen - *The difference between Toulouse-Lautrec and the other Impressionists emerges most clearly in the portraits. He was not attracted to the changing effects of light in nature, preferring instead to dedicate himself to man and the environments created by him.*

10. The Countess Adèle Tapié de Céleyran de Toulouse-Lautrec at the Château de Malromé - 1887. Musée Henri de Toulouse-Lautrec, Albi - *This portrait of his mother shows her in a moment of domestic tranquillity. The details of the setting serve to emphasize the psychological content of the painting.*

11. Cancan - 1896-97. Private collection, Turin - *Toulouse-Lautrec used just a few quick pencil strokes touched up with pastels to bring out the frenetic movement of the French Cancan dancers. For the past few years Lautrec had focused on the essentials of drawing at the expense of colour, much preferring light colours, and his greatest masterpieces of the time are the ones that seem least finished.*

12. Jane Avril dancing - c. 1893. Musée d'Orsay, Paris - *Actress and dancer, Jane Avril was one of Toulouse-Lautrec's greatest friends and also one of his favourite subjects. The painter was attracted to her subtle melancholy, and he responded to her sensitivity and her air of refinement, which was in direct contrast to the other popular stars of the day, especially La Goulue.*

13. Standing Dancer - 1890. Private collection, Paris - *This sketch shows the parsimonious use of colour typical of Toulouse-Lautrec; with just a few basic shades he managed to create a unique sense of space. He increasingly used lighter tones in all of his works.*

14. The Drinker - 1889. Musée Henri de Toulouse-Lautrec, Albi - *This portrait of Suzanne Valadier, one of Toulouse-Lautrec's models from ordinary life, shows his skill in capturing the expression of a complex subject while highlighting just a few selected traits. This work, prepared with the help of a number of sketches, was published in the* Courrier Français, *April 21, 1889.*

15. At the Moulin de la Galette - 1889. Collection of Mr. and Mrs. Lewis L. Coburn, The Art Institute of Chicago - *In this work, the viewer feels as if he is a part of the dancing. Toulouse-Lautrec manages this by placing the viewer in the foreground of the painting, thus filling the void between the viewer and the action. The canvas was presented at the Salon des Indépendants in the same year that it was painted.*

16. Portrait of Samary of the Comédie Française - 1889. Collection J. Laroche, Paris - *This extraordinary work shows the artist's highly personal way of capturing the most significant aspects of his subject's personality, analyzing movements and depicting an atmosphere.*

17. Woman at her Toilette - 1896. Musée d'Orsay, Paris - *The artist called this woman "Solitude" and his special qualities of perception and sensitivity allowed him to capture her deep despair. This is one of the few paintings in which the artist disregards the model's face and presents her from the back, seated, stripped to the waist with her red hair gathered in a knot at the nape of her neck.*

18. Woman in Profile - 1895. Private collection, Paris - *This work is one of a series painted during the 1890s; it is a prime example of Lautrec's extraordinary skill in capturing the subject's personality with just a few rapid, precise and certain lines. "There is only the figure," he once said Maurice Joyant, "the landscape is, and must be, merely an accessory."*

19. La Goulue Entering the Moulin Rouge - 1892. Museum of Modern Art, gift of Mrs. David M. Levy, New York - *Toulouse-Lautrec's genius for poster design contributed to La Goulue's immense success and popularity, placing her exuberant image on every street-corner in Paris.*

20. The Englishman at the Moulin Rouge - 1892. Metropolitan Museum of Art, gift of Miss Adelaide Milton de Groot, New York - *This drawing is a wonderful example of the wealth of psychological studies that Toulouse-Lautrec left us. Each one of these studies captures a different facet of human nature. This one shows Mr Warner with two unidentified companions.*

21. The Quadrille Begins - 1892. Musée du Louvre, Paris - *The second of two panels painted for what La Goulue called her "shack"; here the dancer is shown in the foreground among her friends. This has the effect of drawing the viewer into the painting. When the "indigenous quadrille" began, the elegant public took its place at the tables, leaving the floor to the professionals.*

22. Jane Avril Leaving the Moulin Rouge - 1892. Wadsworth Atheneum, Hartford (Connecticut) - *When her popularity, which had been boosted by the artist's many posters, drawings and lithographs of her, faded, Jane Avril was practically cast out of the Moulin Rouge. In this drawing the artist intensified the sense of pathos by immersing his subject in a halo of light.*

23. At the Moulin Rouge - 1892. The Art Institute of Chicago - *There is a story behind each individual at this famous club, the Moulin Rouge: the club habitués on the left, La Goulue, a local dancer with her back to the mirror, and a young girl on the right, wrapped in a shimmering bluish light.*

24. Dance at the Moulin Rouge - 1890. Henry McLhenny Collection, Philadelphia - *Toulouse-Lautrec powerfully conveyed the atmosphere of the Moulin Rouge in this painting. He makes us feel his attraction for the dancers, artists and habitués who mingle together here. Valentin-le-Désossé (Valentin the double-jointed) is shown in the middle of the dance floor with La Goulue. In the background, the man with the white beard has been identified as the painter's father.*

25. The Clowness Cha-U-Kao - 1895. Collection Oskar Reinhart am Römerholz, Winterthur - *The seductive and vivacious figure of Cha-U-Kao dominates the scene in this perfectly constructed composition. The chromatic balance is extraordinary, with the contrast of yellow and brown in the foreground, and the pink gown to the right, which stands out against the intense colours of the background.*

26. La Goulue Waltzing - 1894. Musée Henri de Toulouse-Lautrec, Albi - *At twenty-six, Lautrec began producing posters and his fame spread rapidly for his revolutionary style. All his life he ignored the "belle peinture" style and, as this work shows, focused on capturing realistic images.*

27. Moulin Rouge, La Goulue - 1891. Musée Henri de Toulouse-Lautrec, Albi - *In this poster, as in many of his works, the artist makes the viewer feel a part of the scene that he is observing. This effect is achieved with the dancer's profile in the foreground, which draws the viewer into the world depicted.*

28. Yvette Guilbert - 1894. Musée Henri de Toulouse-Lautrec, Albi - *Though at first the actress did not appreciate the interest the artist showed in her, Lautrec dedicated an entire series of posters to Yvette Guilbert, which contributed greatly to her success. She later began to value the friendship of the artist, as well as the fact that his brilliant style of representation offered a highly subtle interpretation of her personality.*

29. Yvette Guilbert Bowing to her Public - 1894. Musée Henri de Toulouse-Lautrec, Albi - *Toulouse-Lautrec met the actress in 1894 and remained an unflagging admirer of her prodigious talent, her ironic wit and her ability to strike up friendships with all sorts of people. He studied her at length and did a number of portraits of her in an effort to convey the disturbing enigma of her personality.*

30. Dr Gabriel Tapié de Céleyran - 1894. Musée Henri de Toulouse-Lautrec, Albi - *In this portrait of his cousin, the artist enhanced his characteristic economy of line with a new use of colour. When he did this portrait, he had just exhibited in the Salon de la Libre Esthétique, in Brussels, and Arsène Alexandre, editor-in-chief of "Le Rire", invited him to be a regular contributer to the review.*

31. In Bed - 1892. Musée d'Orsay, Paris - *This singularly simple work shows Toulouse-Lautrec's fascination with the private side of people's lives, as opposed to the passionate attachment to nature typical of most Impressionists. His search for the natural led him to the brothels starting in 1891, and he even lived in them for periods of time, in order to better capture the atmosphere.*

32. "Is it Enough to Want Something Passionately?" (The Good Jockey), published in the «Figaro Illustré», July 1895 - *In a period of intense productivity lasting from 1890 to 1900, Toulouse-Lautrec contributed a number of illustrations to periodicals and books, of which this is one example. It was an illustration for R. Coolus' play "The Good Jockey".*

33. Chocolat Dancing at Achille's Bar - 1896. Musée Henri de Toulouse-Lautrec, Albi - *Presented as part of a group of works describing the spontaneous pleasures and the sensational world of Montmartre, this drawing is fascinating for the mixed emotion of vitality and nervous tension that it captures. The viewer shares in this intensity.*

34. Madame Poupoule at her Dressing Table - 1899. Musée Henri de Toulouse-Lautrec, Albi - *This splendid work shows the artist's fully matured talent in terms of his use of colours, as well as of his exceptional sensitivity towards the subject and the setting. The composition's harmony is entirely based upon the relationships between the warm colours of the cylindrical box in the foreground and those of the dressing table in the background.*

35. Marcelle Lender Dancing the Bolero in "Chilpéric" - c. 1897, J.H. Whitney Collection, New York - *Toulouse-Lautrec was so taken with Marcelle Lender's performance in the operetta "Chilpéric" that he returned each night to the theatre to paint her during the show. He did hundreds of studies and sketches that reflect the explosive rhythm and colours of her dance.*

36. The Moorish Dance or the Egyptian Dancing Girls - 1895. Musée d'Orsay, Paris - *This poster of La Goulue dancing under the heat of the Moulin Rouge's stagelights was one of the artist's most celebrated works, though his critics maintained that his success and that of the café-concert owed everything to the fame of its performers.*

37. The Dance of La Goulue and Valentin-le-Désossé - 1895. Musée du Louvre, Paris - *Toulouse-Lautrec's great talent lays in his ability to render pathos with a vibrant and exciting style. This work is filled with all the people he loved — dancers, singers, and actors. The effect of this contrast in his posters and theatre bills is what made him so popular.*

38. In the Salon, Rue des Moulins - 1894. Musée Henri de Toulouse-Lautrec, Albi - *Of the many works by Toulouse-Lautrec inspired by life in the "maisons", this is the most striking. The spacious salon with its violent colours is permeated with a dense, almost suffocating atmosphere. The rigid figure of the "madame", with her sharply rendered facial features, is easy to single out among the "girls" lounging on the sofa.*

39. The Unknown Lady Passenger of Cabin 54 - 1896. Lithograph - *Toulouse-Lautrec introduced innovations to the graphic arts and modern advertising that are still valid today. His unusual and direct approach to the subject and his minimal concept of the line and colour still make up part of the modern aesthetic.*

40. The English Barmaid at the "Star" - 1899. Musée Henri de Toulouse-Lautrec, Albi - *The Star was a bar in Le Havre where the artist met the young Englishwoman of this portrait, one of the masterpieces of his last period. In this portrait he reverted to his immediate lines and aggressive colours, deftly filling the background with minimal geometric shapes.*

41. At the Bar: The Customer and the Anemic Cashier - 1898. Kunsthaus, Zurich - *Two anonymous people have been immortalized by the artist's incredibly skilful sketches. With pen and ink Lautrec managed to paint and sketch at the same time. Few characterizations achieve the poignancy of the effect of this florid face, seen here in juxtaposition with the woman's emaciated profile, accentuated by her white jabot.*

42. Messalina Seated - 1900. The Art Institute of Chicago - *Toulouse-Lautrec was delighted with the subjects he found in Bordeaux at the provincial opera house. He painted Mademoiselle Cocyte in Mailhace and Halévy's "La Belle Hélène", and Mademoiselle Ganne in a now-forgotten opera called "Messalina".*

43. The Barroom - 1900. Collection of Mrs. Florence Gould - *Toulouse-Lautrec did this theatre bill in the year before his death. It announces the production of Emile Zola's "L'Assommoir" (The Barroom) at the Théâtre de la Porte Saint-Martin on November 1st, 1900. Lucien Guitry directed the play, and it was he who commissioned the playbill.*

44. An Examination at the Paris Medical School - 1901. Musée Henri de Toulouse-Lautrec, Albi - *Started just months before his death, this is the last of his important works. In it, the artist seems to be developing a new technique involving sombre visual masses and dense colours.*

1. *Self-Portrait of Henri de Toulouse-Lautrec* - 1880. Musée Henri de Toulouse-Lautrec, Albi

2. *The Mail-Coach* - 1881. Musée du Petit Palais, Paris

3. *The Countess Adèle de Toulouse-Lautrec at Malromé* - 1883. Musée Henri de Toulouse-Lautrec, Albi

4. *Tethered Horse* - c. 1881. Private collection, Paris

5. *At the Circus Fernando: the Ringmaster* - 1880. The Art Institute of Chicago

6. *The Laundress* - 1889. Private collection, Paris

7. *Girl with Red Hair* - 1889. Bührle Collection, Zurich

8. *The Painter Henri Rachou* - c. 1882.
Algur H. Meadows Collection, Dallas

9. *Portrait of Hélène Vary* - 1888. Kunsthalle, Bremen

10. *The Countess Adèle Tapié de Céleyran de Toulouse-Lautrec at the Château de Malromé* - 1887. Musée Henri de Toulouse-Lautrec, Albi

11. *Cancan* - 1896-97. Private collection, Turin

12. *Jane Avril Dancing* - c. 1893. Musée D'Orsay, Paris

13. *Standing Dancer* - 1890. Private collection, Paris

14. *The Drinker* - 1889. Musée Henri de Toulouse-Lautrec, Albi

15. *At the Moulin de la Galette* - 1889. Collection of Mr. and Mrs. Lewis L. Coburn, The Art Institute of Chicago

16. *Portrait of Samary of the Comédie Française* - 1889. Collection J. Laroche, Paris

17. *Woman at her Toilette* - 1896. Musée d'Orsay, Paris

18. *Woman in Profile* - 1895. Private collection, Paris

19. *La Goulue Entering the Moulin Rouge* - 1892. Museum of Modern Art,
    gift of Mrs. David M. Levy, New York

20. *The Englishman at the Moulin Rouge* - 1892. Metropolitan Museum of Art, gift of Miss Adelaide
Milton de Groot, New York

21. *The Quadrille Begins* - 1892. Musée du Louvre, Paris

22. *Jane Avril Leaving the Moulin Rouge* - 1892. Wadsworth Atheneum, Hartford (Connecticut)

23. *At the Moulin Rouge* - 1892. The Art Institute of Chicago

24. *Dance at the Moulin Rouge* - 1890. Henry McLhenny Collection, Philadelphia

25. *The Clowness Cha-U-Kao* - 1895. Collection Oskar Reinhart am Römerholz, Winterthur

26. *La Goulue Waltzing* - 1894. Musée Henri de Toulouse-Lautrec, Albi

27. *Moulin Rouge, La Goulue* - 1891. Musée Henri de Toulouse-Lautrec, Albi

28. *Yvette Guilbert* - 1894. Musée Henri de Toulouse-Lautrec, Albi

29.
*Yvette Guilbert Bowing to her Public* - 1894. Musée Henri de Toulouse-Lautrec, Albi

30. *Dr Gabriel Tapié de Céleyran* - 1894. Musée Henri de Toulouse-Lautrec, Albi

31. *In Bed* - 1892. Musée d'Orsay, Paris

32. *"Is it Enough to Want Something Passionately?"* (The Good Jockey), *published in the "Figaro Illustré",
   July 1895*

33. *Chocolat Dancing at Achille's Bar* - 1896. Musée Henri de Toulouse-Lautrec, Albi

34. *Madame Poupoule at her Dressing Table* - 1899. Musée Henri de Toulouse-Lautrec, Albi

35. *Marcelle Lender Dancing the Bolero in "Chilpéric"* - c. 1897. J.H. Whitney Collection, New York

36. *The Moorish Dance or the Egyptian Dancing Girls* - 1895. Musée d'Orsay, Paris

37. *The Dance of La Goulue and Valentin-le-Désossé* - 1895. Musée du Louvre, Paris

38. *In the Salon, Rue des Moulins* - 1894.
Musée Henri de Toulouse-Lautrec, Albi

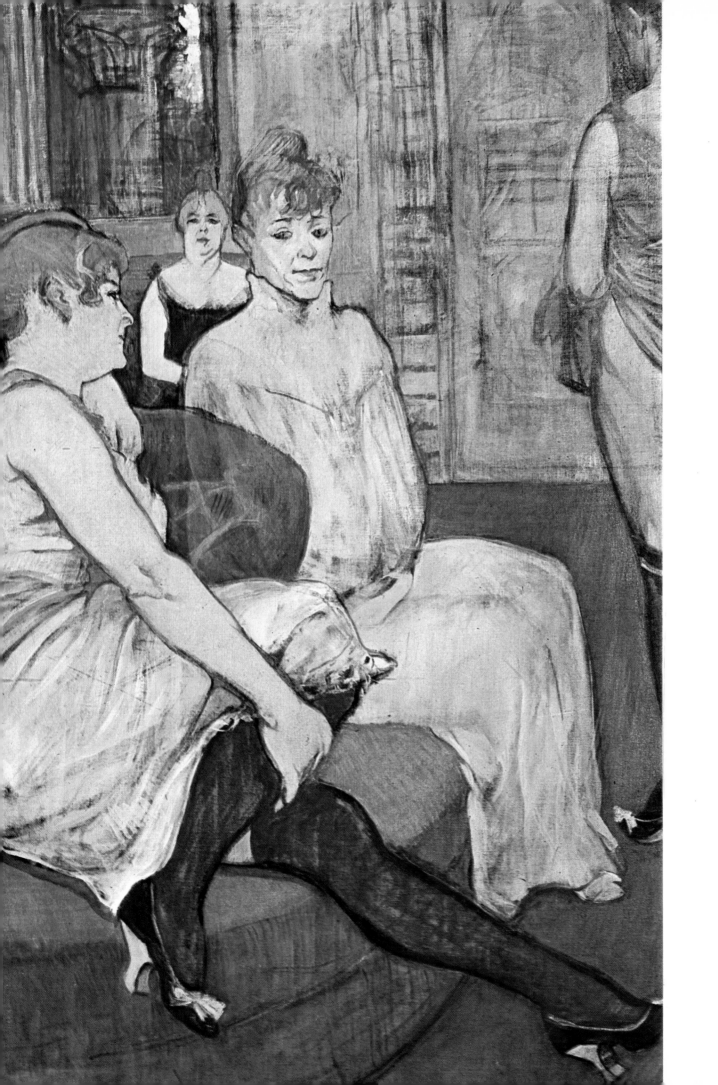

39. *The Unknown Lady Passenger of Cabin 54* - 1896. Lithograph

40. *The English Barmaid at the "Star"* - 1899. Musée Henri de Toulouse-Lautrec, Albi

41. *At the Bar: The Customer and the Anemic Cashier* - 1898. Kunsthaus, Zurich

42. *Messalina Seated* - 1900. The Art Institute of Chicago

43. *The Barroom* - 1900. Collection of Mrs. Florence Gould

44. *An Examination at the Paris Medical School* - 1901. Musée Henri de Toulouse-Lautrec, Albi

*Editor in chief* Anna Maria Mascheroni

*Art director* Luciano Raimondi

*Text* Deanna Valente Bernar

*Translation* Carol Rathman

*Production* Art, Bologna

*Photo Credits* Gruppo Editoriale Fabbri S.p.A., Milan

Copyright © 1988 by Gruppo Editoriale Fabbri S.p.A., Milan

Copyright © 1990 by PHIDAL
for the Canadian edition

ISBN 2-89393-046-8

Printed in Italy by Gruppo Editoriale Fabbri S.p.A., Milan